Get **more** out of libraries

Please return or renew this item by the last date shown.
You can renew online at www.hants.gov.uk/library
Or by phoning 0845 603 5631

Hampshire
County Council

A Passage from Afar
(Collected Verse)

Bradley J Barnes

authorHOUSE®

AuthorHouse™ UK Ltd.
500 Avebury Boulevard
Central Milton Keynes, MK9 2BE
www.authorhouse.co.uk
Phone: 08001974150

First published by AuthorHouse   4/16/2010

ISBN: 978-1-4490-9154-5 (sc)

CO15406954
08/14

Printed in the United States of America
Bloomington, Indiana

This book is printed on acid-free paper.

If you have to ask what poetry is?
You'll never know.

Illustrated by
Rachel Wellstead.

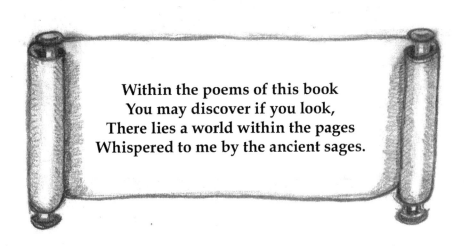

Within the poems of this book
You may discover if you look,
There lies a world within the pages
Whispered to me by the ancient sages.

Dedicated to
Pamela Ann Knight

A Poem for a Lonely Night

Sitting lonely in the night
Thoughts conducted by candlelight,
A light that flickers pure as gold
Which leaves you calm complete and whole,
Stare stare, into God's eye
Life for once will pass you by.

Sitting lonely in the night
Time ticks by out of sight,
The night has come to cleanse the day
To give it rest and hide its ray,
Forgive life's trouble and her pains
Cast them off while you remain.

Sitting lonely in the night
You're inner Soul burning bright,
The candlelight has gone out
The room is dark, you have no doubt,
Sleep sleep, call the ghosts of time
As you leave the earth for one last time.

The Torch of Love

The Torch of Love is a burning flame
That burns so bright it consumes all pain,
Light the torch, it will burn bright
A burning flame, day and night.

Ignorance is Bliss

God said, 'Can't you see the stars!'
'Look at the beauty, not just the scars',
'And tell me truly, children of earth'
'Is that too much to ask for birth!'

Father's Prayer

His voice buried beyond in dreams
Where two are one in beauty serene,
A different world, he awaits me now
As we now know the Divide so well.

(for John Barnes – see you soon)

Dr💧p of Rain

A rain drop falls amongst the trees
That disappears within the breeze,
The grass absorbs, no visible trace
Giving life, the hidden face.

Fright Night (Part 1)

Endless dreams that stalk the dark
Ghouls, ghosts and wolves that bark,
Creatures lurking in big parks
They hound your sleep, your life and lark.

Dear Mum

There is a Mum who is so kind
And to see her face pleased my mind,
Her beauty immune, lost of pride
Behind her love it could not hide.

(for Pamela Ann Knight – I love you!)

Saturday Man

Saturday night he's a disco man
A single suit, a one-night stand,
He drinks the drinks and lives for fun
But what is left when it's all done.

Half a Loaf of Revolution

I demand a revolution,
I'll plan it with great execution,
We'll get the same old class on top,
Why not go halfway and stop!

Explorer's Hope

Great distance reaching to the sky
You dash the hopes in a critic's eye,
Wherever you look and dare aspire,
Only a brave hand seizes the fire.

(for Mathew Flinders – seven years was just too long!)

Horizon of Hearts

As I opened my heart my horizon grew
As my horizon grew my heart did too,
Heart to horizon, horizon to heart
Opened and grew, what's to tell them apart?

Who are you Praying to?

My mind is a burning hell,
And my heart apart as well,
I pray, beg ask and cry,
To a deaf, dumb and blind God who won't reply.

Men of Truth

They didn't come to conceal it,
They came to reveal it
The true and living God, the sons – man,
And if you ever need assistance, take their hand.

(for Tony Ashenden - forever debted)

Medusa

Snakes in hair that covers her bones
Piercing eyes turn flesh to stone,
Eye to eye, stare at her glare
An eternal statue lost, hidden within her lair.

Judgement Day

We sinners that labour in the dumb
Soon to perish when judgement comes,
Patience of 2000 years, the task
Hidden behind society's mask.

The Eighth Day

There came a day the sky went dark, the world began to change,
The eternal garden did not grow, the air it tasted strange,
A shifting toxic current brought a spreading blight
And every single life form simply vanished overnight.

Life's a Shadow

Life's a shadow over grass
That we just seem to pass,
The shadow lost like sunset
When life is known and death is met.

The Conditioning Room

Please rescue kids from maths and prisms
False ideals, ideologies and isms,
Better develop natural talent and arts
Or else you are nursing bleeding hearts.

Jackie's Cross

Don't be cross, Jackie
Jackie, don't be cross,
For when your cross Jackie,
Then the world becomes a loss.

The Sound of One Hand Clapping

Listen very carefully!

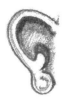

Heart's Breath

The heart breathes love that gives devotion,
Stronger than shore, wind and ocean,
It gives to all from one position
An endless pore, in repetition.

The Mystical Quest

Symbols are not what they seem,
Life will forever unfold,
Making the unseen seen
Making the unreal told.

(for Sufism)

The Gateless Gate

The gift of self is a sacred right
Where one can rise above all heights,
For only the few have ever trod
I therefore abdicate to God.

(for Clive – God Bless You)

Man Created God

God created man
To create himself,
There is nothing to understand
Only believe in yourself.

(for Karl Marx)

Bass Strait

The strength of wave ocean rolls
That be, indifferent to consume a soul,
Windy cold warm and wet
When on Bass Strait I beset.

(for George Bass)

Don't look back
unless you intend going that way!

The Balled of Mr Mean

There was a man who was so mean
Who folk avoided, he was so mean,
He did not care, he loved his days
Blind to give and share Gods praise,
Kept out of sight, out of mind
Unaware he was so blind,
To be so mean and so satisfied
Made the Angels weep and cry,
And in the world had not a friend
Throughout his life until the end.

Oh what a terrible fate it is
To have to live a life like this,
He died early one Christmas Day,
And was not found until mid-May,
No-one cared, no air of grief
Nor in the air any sighed relief,
Buried where the grass was green
Never again to be heard or seen,
Dealt a hand that was so unfair
To be born so mean and without a care.

Port Arthur's Pain

Port Arthur's long and tortured pain
Where men were killed or turned insane,
Knowing you were better off dead
Than face Port Arthur, or so they said.
Many men made a chivalrous run,
Against the odds and a baking sun,
But for the most their sanity lost
Immeasurable pain that you could not cost,
Beaten with a man made tool,
Another soul broken, so sad, so cruel.

Many men could not take the strain
Of Port Arthur, this inhuman pain,
One such man was Martin Cash
Who ran three times to escape the lash,
He became a bushranger and stole to live,
Robbing the rich, who had so much to give,
He got re-caught and served his time,
Lasting Port Arthur's terrible crimes,
He won his freedom and settled down,
To live his life, in Hobart Town.

(for Martin Cash)

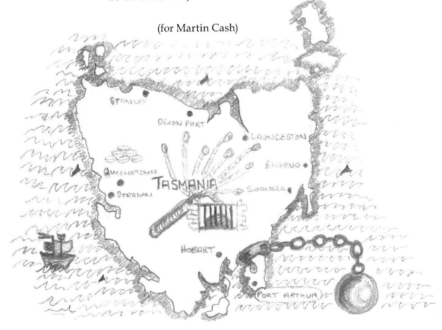

Saint Sinner

Do you want to free your Soul?
Or fill your pockets up with gold,
You only get in Heaven's Gate
If you've practiced love, not hate,
Heaven's a place where one must do
Don't just talk; when, why, who,
So keep that Bible on your shelf
God helps those that help themselves,
Live your life and take its test
Walk the path to happiness.

Don't live your life upon your sleeve
Full of sadness and full of grief,
In a pure heart and a good mind
Love can work and God will find,
But if the answer is suicide
Ask the question – Dr. Jekyll or Mr. Hyde,
As every time a church bell rings
Another Angel gets its wings,
But if you are out of reach and out of touch
You'll be the patrol saint of nothing much.

(for John Bunyan – great book!)

Sorry we're Late Again

Husband waits at the door of the flat,
Coat done up, ready with hat,
He flicks the light, it's dark and shady
Calling his wife, his hesitant lady,
'Were going to be late', time is humming
'So come on darling'. Reply, 'I'm coming',
She walks down the hall in wild distress
'I hate this colour', I'll change my dress',
All alone at the door again, patience tested,
He turns to anger, and becomes infested.

'The taxi's here', our waiting lift,
Shouting again he becomes more miffed,
'Come on, come on', he stands there snarling
'We're going to be late, hurry darling',
Another colour matched, a dress she chooses
As all his patience now he loses,
Arriving late, with curtain rose on the show,
Their seats positioned in the middle of the row,
Crawling and climbing like sorry factors
Sorry we're late again, disrupting audience and actors.

I Need to Travel

I need to travel, travel I will
From Southsea Pier to Portsdown Hill.

I need to travel, travel I say
From Marble Bar to Wine Glass Bay.

I need to travel, travel the lands
From oceans great to distant sands.

I need to travel, travel I do
From in to out and all the way through.

I need to travel, travel I shall
From the Gates of Heaven to the depths of Hell.

I need to travel, travel I must
From celibacy to endless lust.

I need to travel
I need to travel
I need to travel
I need to travel
I need to travel
I need to travel
I need to travel
I need to travel

In Memorial

Here lies a beautiful lady
Beside the oak bright and shady,
Loved in life for her heart of gold
Asleep now beneath the moonlight cold:

Her beauty stays, her love I kept
As I see the oak where she slept,
I'm rusting now, there is **no dan**cing
For here I'm left empty at her passing.

Third Eye Blind

Is death wrong? Or are we blind
To see this world and miss God's mind.
For beyond two eyes there lies a third
Where death is known, seen and heard.

We're sinking as the light lives on,
In God's mind far beyond,
Look down deep, from the heart
Beyond this world where Heaven starts:

Huon Highway

We travelled south of Hobart, hands on the wheel,
Shaking in our hire car, a trembling lump of steel.
Bags in back, as the tyres burn the bitumen grey,
Kicking up a red dust swirl, along the Huon Highway.

We crossed bridged creeks built of old, that seem so new,
And here and there a Tasmanian devil, and a little kangaroo,
The sun is baking, and we missed that slight chance of rain,
As we drove off in the distance across the open plain.

(for Ben Leigh – a great day!)

The Walker

I walk through sun to overcasting
I walk alone, everlasting,
I walk up maintains, I tread the sand
I'm always walking, I never stand.

I walk along, full of smiles
Step by step many miles,
Through the streets, an odd alleyway
Of every year of everyday.

Reclaiming our Roots

I once had a head full of hair
That went thin and now is bare,
Found a wig which I bought
But people laughed and my wife got distraught.

Be bald and proud there is no shame
Losing your hair it's part of the game,
There's nothing wrong with a head of skin
It's what's inside of the outer rim.

Cycle of-life

Arise all you men,
Only to fall again,
Aspire and entrust,
Matter turns to dust.

Under your stone,
Heavens ladder is thrown,
Climbing out unbound,
Cycle begins again – around.

Young Minds Failed

And many a nightly hour does bring
Packs of young'uns loitering,
To me who sees – then writes the tales
On why and how society fails.

With no hope left that they can strive
Clearly known in their shallow lives,
Youth now burst in their years despite,
For growing older must bring delight!

O'Little Man

Look at yourself O'little man
Your time is up, it is outran,
You don't have that which you can't buy
It's out of reach of ear and eye.

Outward happiness, no inward joy
You know so much, you think old boy,
How you struggle within your shell
Living your life in an empty cell.

The Kookaburra

The Bushmen's clock laughs at noon
They laugh in chorus not in tune,
Perched above in trees so high
Hidden behind their laughing cry.

As the night begins to creep
This laughing bird awakes from sleep,
From tree to tree and through your door,
Their sound becomes a jungles roar.

Come Dance with Me

Whatever I do I do it right
And you can dance with me on a Saturday night,
Whatever I touch it turns to gold
I drink, smoke, lust and never grow old.

I've turned pearls and diamonds into sand
I have millions like you in the palm of my hand,
I'm the master of pain, suffering and death
Let me into your heart and I'll reap your flesh.

Mother Earth

Please listen, and don't be surprised,
A lot is hidden from our human eyes,
Extinction, destruction; **'PLEASE THAT'S ENOUGH'**
For Mother Earth isn't all that tough.

When all her beauty becomes so stained,
That we're unable to right it again
Then let's act now and protect her fast,
For her springtime beauty cannot last.

(for William Ricketts)

Mount Wellington

Climbing up Mt Wellington, clomping inch by inch
Resting on the summit, then cross the snow capped pinch,
Venturing down, on track running high,
Seeing far below, as we're cut against the sky.

The hopes and achievement that we share,
'Move on, move on', and drink the mountain air,
Aching-bodies, pain soon left behind
As we beat Mt Wellington, life's memory in our minds.

(for Charles Barnes – many thanks!)

Marriage for One

A life for two in a silk-lined carriage,
Two Souls as one in a perfect marriage,
But looming far in future's air
The carriage is stopping at the town of despair.

The spoke wheels long past the empty church
Misty promises faded, beyond a birch,
The candle of their love burns cold
In a carriage for one where two cannot hold.

Experience – The Great Teacher

The hardest teacher of them all
Is experience, which stands so tall,
The test comes first, the lesson later,
And then our knowledge is far greater.

Take the test and you will know
Through its knowledge you'll always grow,
Feel the fear, go through with it,
Now the courage of your self is lit.

A Time for Change

The trouble with politicians
Is we all have suspicions
'Cos they hide their worst positions
In a world of tough decisions:

And after all the voting
If we lick off the sugar coating
You'll see their laughing and their bloating
Because they've had us and they're gloating.

Limits of Time

Beginnings are not known
It's a loss – the first day,
From what has come and grown
Each moment moves away.

For we would give much
To see at close hand
First sight first touch,
And even what is planned.

Money Talks

I've got an eye to see with,
And an ear to hear with,
I've got a mouth to talk with,
And a nose to smell with.

I've got a hand to touch with,
And legs to walk with,
I've got a stomach to eat with,
And lungs to breathe with.

But I have no smiles, through life's miles,
For without cash I am devoid.

I'd swap my health, for just some wealth,
For without cash I am destroyed.

For I have nothing to see,
Nothing to hear,
No-one to talk with,
And nothing to smell.

Nothing to touch,
Nowhere to walk,
Nothing to eat,
Only bad air to breathe.

*The Master

Great darkness came over the earth; Joseph of Arimethea lit a torch of sprouse,
He passed down from the hill into the valley, for he had business in his own house.
Kneeling on the flint stones of the Valley of Desolation, he saw a man,
The man was naked; weeping his hair was the colour of honey, his body a white tan.

The young man had wounded his body with a crown of thorns, blood run over his toes,
And he who had great possessions said to the young man, tell me of your woes.
"I do not wonder that your sorrow is so great, he was more than a man",
"It is not for Him I am weeping, but for me".

"I too have changed water into wine, healed the sick, and given sight to those who could not see",
"I too have walked upon water, cast out devils, and given food to the hungry",
"I too have raised the dead, and made men free",
"All things He has done I have done also, and yet they have not crucified me".

The Astral Sermon

See the guardians of immortality,
Awareness is the key to their reality,
Mental, emotional, physical live in harmony,
Wholeness gives the understanding – you'll Be.
So follow the inner star that burns so bright,
Trust the Immortal Masters of Light,
Use the earth time, understand the lesson,
And your passing will be your blessing,
Act as one, don't hesitate,
Truly love thyself, avoid all hate.
Don't live in separation,
Through Being, you'll know the destination.
Knock, it shall be opened unto you,
Walk through the door – grasp the jewel.
They reigneth over all, broodith over all,
Standing by your side, every breath, every call.
Be true to all, to your heart,
Live in the Now, now is the start,
Pray. Ask, and it shall be given
On earth as it is in Heaven.
Give the right food to a soul that is hungry.
Plant a good seed, to become a strong tree,
Give guidance to all who have lost their way
And when your work is done, be still and pray.

(for the uninitiated)

Hidden World beyond Life's Web

The spider spun a web, a painted loom,
Up in the corner of someone's room,
When in came some flies so unaware
Of the web and his invisible lair,
One flew in and one flew wide
As the cobweb shook from side to side.
Help! Help cried the imprisoned fly
And all his friends gave out a sigh.
Out came the spider like a thundering boat
To seize the frightened fly afloat,
The fly froze, then shook with fear
As he heard the spider's victory cheer,
The spider glided with silken sail
Across the web, (the fly's open jail),
He wriggled and cried on the spider's thread
But fate came quick, he was soon dead.
Poor, poor fly, was his life in vain?
To have to suffer such tortured pain,
Should he have lived to sing his songs
Or has he gone to where he belongs,
Back to where we all have came
Where flies and spiders are all the same,
A hidden world beyond life's web
Where all of life live as one and share God's bed.

My Lost Love

I lost my love a time ago
For her I pine and want to know,
Where she is and what she does
(I betrayed our love and God's trust).

For all our years and all the rest
I wish her well and all the best,
I'm paying the price, but she never knows
The pain I feel and all the lows.

My other loves have passed away
But all our times just seem to stay,
It will never pass, her gentle touch,
To think that once we loved so much.

(for Annette Deguara – sorry!)

Gluttony

He stuffed so much - the greedy slob,
His appetite amazed us,
Until he grew into a blob,
And blew his gut to blazes.

He thought of nothing but his meals
And would eat more if known,
We hope his life does but reveal
What danger can be sown.

So eat with care and think below
Consider there's another,
Don't eat so much you grow and blow
And always thank your mother.

While Men Argue Nature Acts

Your time it is a 'flying
Like birds up in the sky,
What is it they are saying!
Listen to us fly.

Your time is rolling in
Like waves upon the shore,
What is it they are saying!
Listen to us roar.

Your time is creeping on
Like vines upon a wall,
What is it they are saying!
Listen even more.

Listen to the wind,
Listen to the sky,
Be at one with nature's mind,
Life won't pass you by.

(for Henry David Thoreau)

The One

The day was just the same, my life was quiet and still,
When I saw her, and with love my heart did fill,
So beautiful, an angel in the flesh, what love,
So filled with hope was I, be mine, O please O Lord above.

Her face, her eyes set me a blaze, my heart began to pound,
This day my life forever changed, the one I had now found,
For I must act, or ever live my deep regret,
Hearing her sweet voice; then O Love my heart did set.

(for The One)

A Warm Australian Christmas

Waking on Christmas Day, silence, it's a Christmas on my own,
Distant family, friends, and thoughts long past of home.
I'm sad, Christmas Day is no friend of mine despite a warming of the sun,
It's about snow, carols, frosted windows, kids and fun.

It's not my age, its Christmas, it's about nostalgia, I think,
Where is all the Christmas feel, TV repeats, unexpected family, food and drink.
At home, its Christmas Day if there's laughs, and unwanted presents,
Love, sharing, family and friends, that's what it is in essence.

(25.12.99 – A sad day)

Inner Priest

Within ourselves there lies a seed
A dormant power who must be freed,
For as the acorn frees the oak
The inner priest from shells awoke.

Inner priest give chance to heal
Allow the heart to truly feel,
As in your dreams you are complete,
In Angel's arms you fall asleep.

For all the power that's deep inside,
For all the pain we try to hide,
Restore your true inheritance
Through giving joy and innocence.

Hippie

The hippie is so mellow
A chirpy happy fellow,
He is friendly and most kind
Say what you will, he doesn't mind.

The hippie knows no shame
And he never casts a blame,
He lives without our cares
With flowered shirts and coloured flares.

He always has a smile
Forever, not a while,
Anger is not his game
That's why hippie is his name.

No Cure for Cancer

He won't give up his cigarettes,
They will kill him he forgets,
He'll die or lose a limb,
So much a part of him.

It serves a false need,
Planting the cancer seed,
But he enjoys it, he'll assert
It's nice and doesn't hurt.

Forgetting his lost pretences,
It's destroying all his senses,
It's not just his money it steals,
Remember - **SMOKING KILLS.**

The Lighthouse

Far along the distant shore,
A light burns bright like never before,
This light is old and wise
And at night nothing can disguise.

Perched high above the sandy dune
Reaching out toward the moon,
Captains know the hidden meaning,
A path to guide them in.

Stretching out into the seas
Cutting the dark through the breeze,
Stopping boats from hitting cliffs
Becoming tales and ancient myths.

Rape

A disaster happened in the night
Her soul is crushed with monstrous fright,
Coming from the poisoned deep
Fears will plague her silent sleep.

God's Heaven seems so far away,
The demon face, this living grey,
People now seen as friend or foe
Through the apocalypse of this woe:

Her heart now knows its fallen doom
That was to happen, the powers that loom,
For this unknowing shock of fate
In Heaven, she will rise more great.

Judo Master

Here is a player he gives his show,
Body ready, his mind aglow,
A mortal coil built to withstand
As he executes his throw in hand.

For a single move his only feel
A focused technique from head to heel,
As mind and body absorbs the strain
Opponent served his awaiting pain.

He grabs the ghi, opponent felt
As a ti-otoshi is quickly dealt,
Opponent thrown for making a lunge
Aggression crushed as he takes his plunge.

(for Bruce Heffer – thanks)

The Female of the Species

You got a wonder-bra, make-up on your face
Knickers and stockings all over the place,
A leather mini with a buckle outside
What you got in there you trying to hide.

You put colour in your hair, contacts in your eyes
You love to shop, but never sure of your size,
Pencilled eyebrows and you walk in high heels
Potion's lotions with all the fancy frills.

What is the ingredient, you seem so hollow
Whatever you are made off I just can't follow,
Sugar and spice was just a bluff,
Can you tell me please what is this stuff.

A Silent Cry

Locked in prison hidden in the street
No sight of justice was he going to meet,
From prison cell to the prison garden
An innocent man, that was not pardoned.

His innocence killed, his mind confused
'Killer killer', they all accused,
Taking his life, it destroyed another
When crucified it killed his mother.

The truth was known, did anyone sound,
No justice from those who are all self-crowned,
Beating inside he might as well be dead
When all was too late, Oh sorry they said.

(for Stefan Kiszko and Charlotte Kiszko – My Love)

Modern Town

Modern town, train station, one day on a train,
Roaring through, there is nothing much to see,
Every modern town that has busy streets will feign
A sight, that struggles between care and apathy.

As the train races past, its hooting seems to mock
The traffic congested, though all the lights show green,
This chaos that clears by about 7 o'clock,
Through those tiny streets, as we race by unseen.

We rock along the track, carriages rolled,
As all the passengers pay their over-priced fare,
'The food and drink is now served', hot and cold,
And this modern town might as well not be there.

A Place of Meaningless Time

There is a place of meaningless time
That we all aspire to, but can never hold,
A place where all are in their prime,
And on instant you know that death destroys old.

There is a place of meaningless time
Filled with the sound of a different vibration,
Timeless travel that we all must climb
Where only time lives in splendid isolation.

There is a place of meaningless time
Where mortal life is destroyed, taken away,
A place, time dormant, of heart-like rhyme,
If only we saw the twilight of such day.

?

It's larger than all knowledge known
It's bigger than all measures,
It's fuller than all food that's sown
And richer than all treasures!

It's happier than all gladness
Its power has no fear,
It's saner than all madness
And braver than a tear!

(for E. Nigma)

The Journeys End

How poor life seems, how vain when we scan
Its lack of depth, I pity man.
But looking into its depth I see
A very important mystery,
For in this depth we all must tend
To find God's divine and given end.

Insomnia

I have bad dreams that plagued my sleep
Awake all night, a conscious heap,
Awake all night, tired all day
Had my soul been cast away,
I sadly reflect with mounting dread
The darkest time lay ahead.

In Two Minds

Would I of,
Or would I not of,
For if I could of,
I would of,
But I shouldn't,
So I didn't.

The Power

Thought's appear, you ponder on
Directions that go far beyond,
When entering into the inner crust,
And falling down, you must entrust,
Apparitions constructed from the mind
Follow them down. A sign divine.

Capitalism, with the Gloves Off
(Economy in a Madhouse)

You dream of wealth and fancy cars
Endless lust and fat cigars,
Boundless greed spoke in cocktail bars
Designer suits, and credit cards,
You're arrogant, you lack all charm
You're hard to swallow and cause much harm.

Human all to Human

To win the battle of life, be tactical,
Be aware and strong, be practical,
Listen from inside, know now
It's up to you to show all how.
And the way to show it is –
'Get rid of dead teachers who don't know enough to know this!'

(for Friedrich Nietzsche)

The Hidden Ones

Do not look in the mirror, it's not true,
And I'm not you, so do what you must do.
Only those with stout hearts will drive and survive.
Men of strong faith that know, and have been sent,
Hearts that give truly, and show love, that is meant.

They live a passionate life, through action not intent,
They see beyond the mirror, without impediment.
Act without delay, they say, walk then pray,
And dare express a love that's bold,
Living and shunning what they are told.

(for Omar Khayyám - who is the potter?)

The Moment

Give yourself to the now,
Don't hold on, let go let go,
Don't ask – who why when and how
Be at one, through now you'll know,
Don't hold on, allow; allow.

Renew yourself everyday
And eternally renew yourself again,
Through love and peace, happy, be gay,
And once you are free, free other men,
Don't stop, free more, sow and reap God's pay.

My Epitaph

A New Day

The greatest evil is but man
Who schemes a horrid nasty plan,
Justifying his plan through God
Excluding his own brotherhood.

Man, yes man, dishonest man,
Who works so hard to his plan,
Working with a disnatured mind
Becoming king tyrant of his kind.

Men of old in Eden knew
That we are no longer true,
Whose Love shall remake too good
God's plan for the brotherhood.

The Divine Plan, the dream that we
Must live through peace and harmony,
When Love is king, his mission true,
Will reign for all, not just a few.

The Longing

My heart has made its mind up
For me there is no other,
My heart has made its mind up
I long to be your lover.

My heart has made its mind up
Long for you I do,
My heart has made its mind up
No one else will do.

My heart has made its mind up
Beauty is all I see,
My heart has made its mind up
I wish you would see me.

My heart has made its mind up
I'll hold you when you cry,
My heart has made its mind up
I'll love you till you die.

Time's Watchful Eye

I watch the man who dies
Mortal, so small in size,
Wishing time would fly
As I watch the man who dies.

I watch the man who dies
For when he dies, he'll arise,
Hiding behind the lies
As I watch the man who dies.

I watch the man who dies
A life with many ties,
But I have no ties, he cries
As I watch the man who dies.

I watch the man who dies
Lost, confused, hidden is your prize,
Happy, I'm not lost, he smiles,
As I watch the man who dies.

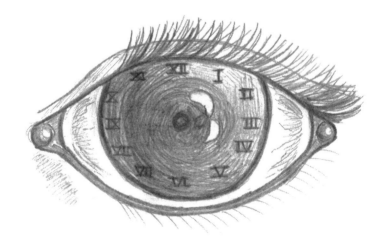

Senator Scam

You elected him in state,
He manipulates your fate,
He's got the motor running,
So heartless, and so cunning.

He wears sheep's clothing,
He lives on fear and loathing,
He's never in your town
At election he's all around.

He is unable to stop,
He lives above the cop,
And while you're counting sheep
He never goes to sleep.

He's always having fun,
Unable to ban the gun!
Living on Champaign and cream,
'God Bless the American Dream'.

Two as One

We hugged around the tree together
In the forest of lush green trees,
The sun shone bright in the summer weather
Two as one in a cooling breeze.

That day I lost an afternoon,
Time forgotten, we could hardly see,
Our love together as a swoon,
Thinking of you and you of me.

Lost in love the minutes hastening
Eyes a-fixed on my world's best friend,
Here together time is not a' wasting,
Through great distance, without end.

We kissed and rolled in the forest as one,
Where love and beauty would reverie,
The perfect melancholy of the sun,
Our love so honest, the world so clear.

(for Camille Lambert – I missed you!)

The Love that Dare not Speak its Name

A poet that moves to the heart never fails
As the heart will steer the written tale,
Oscar Wilde, his beauty gave me the idea
When reading his poems and prose that year.

From my heart I inherited I can tell
He heard The Love from his heart as well,
That when I hear it, as I do,
I know with pride, Wilde heard it to.

A gifted spirit, a contemplative mind,
Living beyond his age, in goal he looked behind,
His heart stolen, he was sacrificed,
Soul broken at the altar, when all denied.

Born with The Love in a hurtful world
Through expression, great beauty unfurled,
Hidden is the power to create and invent,
The wholeness of being is the sole instrument.

(for Oscar Wilde – destroyed by ignorance)

Tiger Snake

A tiger snake hidden in the grass
Walking alone my feet did pass
Unaware of it's nameless dread
Knowing, knowing all the grass it treads.

Taking in the day, so unaware
As the snake stopped with stare,
All I see, its beauty gleams
Going beyond my darkest dreams.

My feelings now are so intense
I'm frozen by its powerful sense,
Eye to eye its trance can hold
Delivering fear for the brave and bold.

Dazzled before it's fixated eye
A step away is my alarmed cry
But knowing it could win the day
It leaves me cold, as it slides away.

The Global Village

Sitting in-front the TV screen
Same old products sold and seen,
Its all propaganda, it's all the same
Continually bombarding your human brain.

Slamming into your fading eyes,
Its power growing more and more in size,
Coming out the TV screen, it will plead,
Cloning the poor in the name of greed.

It sells hamburgers and magazines
Drink, drugs and M16's
Products which destroy us, they are all the same,
People being slain in democracy's name.

Where deceit grazes nothing grows
But artificial life, where no-one sows,
Selling hunger, hurt and so much hate,
Profit for the few in an equal state!

(for Patrick McGoohan – long live No 6)

*Paul

Blinded, the word was spoken
And there he was bound,
The cycle of his life broken
Redemption was all around.

Change, he was commanded
God's touch it seemed so strange,
Damascus the Soul was founded
That embodied his life's change.

Act – The Father told him
And so he began,
Strength that now filled him
With The Love, for man:

Decaying was his body
Before the summon was served,
And now his past speaks sadly
How can all men be saved.

A Passage from Afar contains some of the poems I wish to preserve in print from this period. Since one cannot put poetry through a standard gauge sieve, a principle of selection will always remain variable. So the poems chosen for this collection has come down to freedom of choice and is gleaned from a much larger body of work that is unpublished. The poems owe their existence to many people, times and places. All were written in Australia and span a one year period from November 1999.

Acknowledgements are made to the following. Ben, Dan, James S, Steve, Chris, Jim and James M for being the best of friends. Thanks to Maggie for looking after me. My mum and Fred for being a tower of strength. And I give my thanks in admiration of Tony Ashenden for his genius with whom this would not have been possible. Thanks to Robert Knight for believing in me when others doubted – Individuality is a precious thing.

I would also like to give a special thanks to Charles Barnes for his forbearance in listening, patience, advice and changes on the shape and content of this book, and a place to stay!

My love to Judi, Ariesta, Jo, Christian and John C.
Tasmania and Macquarie Island were beautiful.

Wendy Barnes – RIP.
Ada Winifred Knight – RIP.

To all those who stood fast at Rouke's Drift,
Thermopylae and the JC Slaughter Falls.

Thanks to Rachel for her illustrations, input and enthusiasm.

My Love to all family and friends afar.

"Play Up Pompey"

*Paul is taken from a 10 verse poem entitled
'The Conversion of Paul'.
*The Master was inspired from a story by Oscar Wilde.

Carpe Diem.

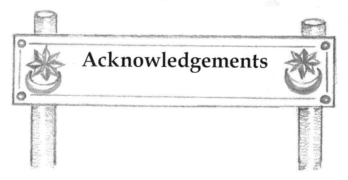

Acknowledgements

Lightning Source UK Ltd.
Milton Keynes UK
UKOW03f1540140514

231693UK00001B/75/P